night maze
paula baysinger morhardt

FOX POINTE PUBLISHING

Dedicated to Grandma Arlene Brinkmeier
and my mother, Mary Baysinger.
Neither one of you ever gave up on me.
I know you are looking down on me, cheering me on.
I hope you are proud.

Copyright © 2020 by Paula Baysinger Morhardt
All rights reserved. Published in the United States by Fox Pointe Publishing, LLP.
No part of this book may be reproduced in any form or by any electronic or
mechanical means, including information storage and retrieval systems,
without permission in writing from the publisher.

www.foxpointepublishing.com/author-paula-morhardt

Library of Congress Cataloging-in-Publication Data
Baysinger Morhardt, Paula, author.
McDowell, Peggy, illustrator.
Farr, Chelsea, designer.
Night Maze. - First edition.
Summary: Part of a collection of poetry born out of tremendous personal loss,
  this volume focuses on the unanswerable questions of life.
ISBN 978-1-9525670-1-8 (hardcover)
1. Poetry. 2. Philosophy. 3. Grief & Healing.
Library of Congress Control Number: 2020908029

Printed and bound in the United States by Lakeside Press Inc.
First printing May 2020

GIVING BIRTH	1
MONSTERS UNDER THE BED	2
THE MARINES HAVE TAKEN MY BABY	5
VICTIMS ALONE	6
JUNE BUGS	9
GOOD JOKES, GOOD STORIES	10
NOT YET READY	13
LOST AND FOUND	14
THE CHILDREN	17
MORE WOLVES	18
LOSING YOU	21
SATURDAY NIGHT	22
WONDERING ON WANDERING	25
FOREVER MISSING YOU	26
DREAM DESTROYED	29
FIRST SNOWFALL	30
CABIN FEVER	33
WHAT IS LEFT	34
TIME	37
REMEMBERING THE PAST	38
TWILIGHT IS A STRANGE LIGHT	40
A MOTHER'S QUESTIONS	42
CROWDED	45

GIVING BIRTH

There were lights in the sky last night.
Someone said it was the aurora borealis.
I do not know.
They rippled and undulated across the sky,
Belly dancing into our retinas.
We oohed and ahhed, and then the rest
went back inside.
I stayed outside,
In the cold,
Watching the lights.
I think it was the sky
giving birth to a new rainbow.

MONSTERS UNDER THE BED

There are monsters under the bed.
I hear them at night
and sometimes during the day.
They don't make a sound
until I'm alone,
But I know they're there.
I find parts of them lying around,
Disguised as old sneakers
and mismatched socks.
I think one of them died
recently
because I found a crumpled-up pair of pants
that didn't belong to anyone in the house.
They don't seem to hurt anything,
Only my nerves.
They hide in the closet sometimes,
And when the door is open, there they are,
In plain sight, concealed as clothes hangers.
The cat can see them,
And follows them with her eyes when they cross the room,
Invisible.

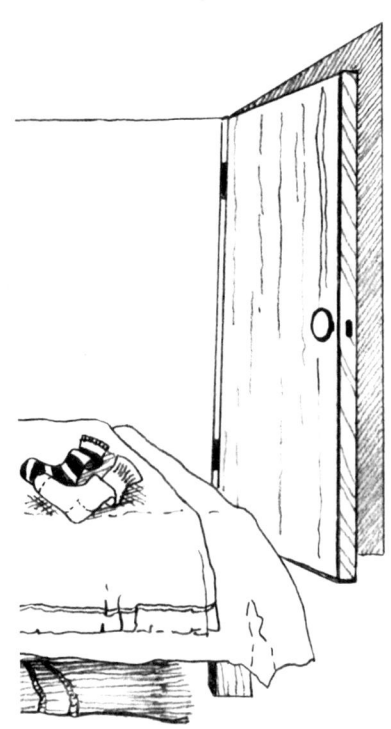

Sometimes the children pretend to hear them
moaning and whining.
The children call out to me,
And I look in the closet and under the bed,
But there's nothing there.
I make a big show of shooing them out,
And I leave a light on.
I hear their soft laughter as I leave the room.
Sometimes, when I clean under the bed,
They grab the broom.
I leave it lying on the floor
and come back for it later.
At night, when I get out of bed,
I make sure and step away quickly,
Just in case.
And I never, ever leave the closet door open
at night.
My family doesn't understand
why I do these things.
They don't know about the monsters.

THE MARINES HAVE TAKEN MY BABY

My son left for the coast today.
His father said, like all the men in the family,
"It'll be the making of him."
My sister-in-law (who has girls) said,
"Think of all the places he'll visit!"
The old folks talk proudly of him
"serving his country."
My best friend, who also has boys, just
pats my hand, understanding.
What is this Marines thing?
Where did it come from?
When did my little boy stop playing
in the sandbox and start
playing with tanks?
I don't understand it, but
I tell him I'll support him.
I'll write cheerful letters,
and send cookies,
and cry happy when he comes home.

And cry when he doesn't.

VICTIMS ALONE

Their eyes glitter with suppressed outrage,
Muscles quiver with violence leashed.
What have we done to warrant this anger?
What have we said to make them turn from us?
We are who we are, no more or less.
Because we are different, they revile us,
Throw stones in their minds.
If this was not a civilized world,
Would they not throw the stones in fact?
We harm no one with our beliefs,
Yet they call us spawn of Satan.
We do not harm their children,
Yet they take ours away from us.
We try to earn our living,
Yet they burn our homes and shops.
Until they turned from us, they were our friends,
our neighbors.
We helped them when they were ill,
Cooked and cleaned and listened to their fears.
Now we are their fears.
We have not changed, only what they know of us.
Will we not find a home? A place where we can be safe?
A sanctuary from the world?
Until we find our home, we must wander,
Enduring their barbed slings and hidden anger.
Knowing the reality, yet unable to live it.
Who will represent us to the outraged?
Who will speak for us?
Who will stand with us?
No one answers, no one comes forth.
We are alone,
Except for ourselves.

JUNE BUGS

They fly at me,
These small tanks in the night.
Their buzz is annoying,
And frightening when heard around your head.
They fly at the light,
Trying to reach the sun in their small minds.
I can relate.

GOOD JOKES, GOOD STORIES

When I die,
I expect to be respected,
But not mourned.
I don't want sad faces to be the last thing I see
as I go off to see the world.
Don't cry, or speak in hushed voices.
Laugh, sing, dance, tell stories.
I will stick around a while
to hear stories.
Tell jokes, but make them good –
I won't stay for bad jokes.
And when time has passed,
And you think of me,
Think of me fondly,
As someone who
loved a good story
and told good jokes.

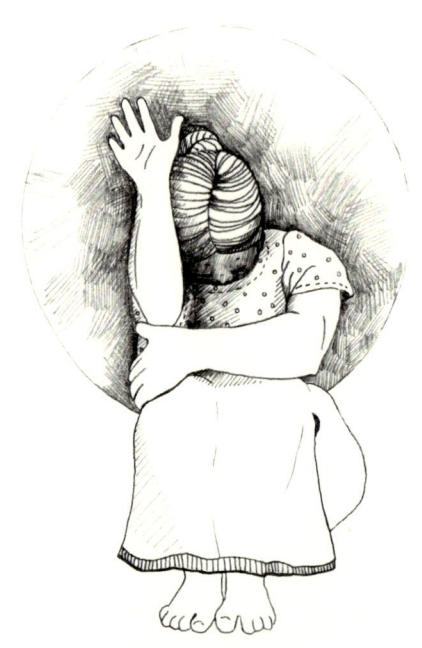

NOT YET READY

When you say I am beautiful,
Please know that I cannot believe it.
I am so scarred,
So broken,
In so many pieces.
I cannot believe anyone could ever find me
beautiful.
Not anymore.
I have been through too much;
Too much life,
Too much pain,
Too much sorrow.
Give me time to
learn to live.
Give me time to
learn to believe.
Give me time to
learn to laugh again.
Maybe, at some time,
I will be ready
to do it again.
Not yet ready,
No,
Not yet.

LOST AND FOUND

Today I lost my reason.
It hadn't far to go before it got away.
I believe it will return some day,
But not soon.

Today I lost my maturity.
It seemed a good idea at the time.
People look at me strangely now,
But look away when they see me looking back.

Today I lost my sanity.
One moment there,
The next not.
I hadn't been using it much lately.

Today I lost my life.
I hovered around awhile,
But nothing was going on,
So I went looking for some things
I had lost.

THE CHILDREN

The children do not understand
and the adults cannot tell them.
Why is the world the way it is?
Why is there anger?
Why is there pain?
The children ask,
But no one answers.
Better they should ask the wind,
Or the waves that lap on the shore.
Perhaps the wolves howl the answer,
Or the reply is whispered in the fire.
Maybe the salmon leaping the rocks know
but aren't telling.
Possibly the old oak,
Standing on the hill,
Could enlighten them.
But not the adults.
If they once knew the answer,
They have lost it.
It was misplaced in the turmoil
of day-to-day living.
It vanished the day
mankind stopped thinking of others
and started thinking only of himself.
There is no one to teach the children
the answer.
No one to teach them how to live,
How to die.
They must go on in ignorance,
Fearing what they do not know,
And fearing the fear.

MORE WOLVES

I heard wolves howling last night.
It stirred something deep inside me.
I wasn't sure if I should be scared or not
because it was a good feeling.
Wolves bring forth that primeval something
lost in the depths of my soul.
Perhaps we need more wolves in the world.
Wolves are good caretakers,
Caring for not only their own young,
But others' as well.
They take only what they need,
And do not waste what they are given.
Some night I will give in to this feeling
and howl back.
We need more wolves in the world.

LOSING YOU

When you started school,
I cried.
I thought I was
losing you.
When you got your license,
I cried.
I thought I was
losing you.
When you started dating,
I cried.
I thought I was
losing you.
Now you're an adult;
You're all grown up and
I'm crying because
I'm losing you.

SATURDAY NIGHT

I sit and I wait.
When he left, he promised
"By eleven, hon."
Ten-thirty he calls:
"Be a bit late –
I've got my quarter down,
but there's a few ahead of me..."
At midnight I go to bed filled,
Not with longing,
(not after four years),
But with aloneness.
A four-year-old and sixteen-month-old
aren't good company.
Nor is the washing machine,
The drainer full of just-washed dishes,
Or the floor I've scrubbed three times,
Waiting.
The cat doesn't talk, and the
TV gets on my nerves.
God,
I wish I were young again.
I feel so old, sometimes ancient.
After all, I'm twenty-one
already.

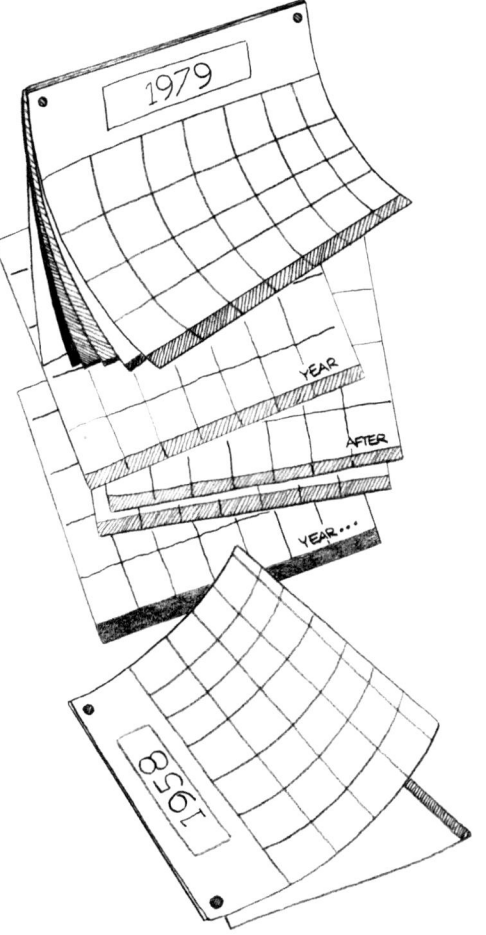

WONDERING ON WANDERING

I wander the house, wondering.
I wonder, am I wandering because I overslept this morning
and can't fall asleep?
I wonder, am I wandering because I am getting old
and sleep is no longer the old friend it once was?
Or am I wandering because you are no longer here?
No longer here to say,
"Come to bed, I'll hold you until you fall asleep."
I wander the house, wondering.

FOREVER MISSING YOU

Just when I think I am coming to a good resolution,
I find something of yours.
Today it was a shirt that hadn't yet been washed,
And it smelled like you.
The wave came crashing down,
And I fell to the floor, wiped off my feet.
I hold it close, smelling you,
Remembering you.
I can hardly breathe, the pain is so great.
How can one person hold this much grief, I wonder.
How can one human body contain this pain?
And then I realize one body cannot, and I open my mouth,
Letting the pain out in stops and starts,
Gasping for air in between,
Keening my pain, wailing my grief,
Sobbing my confusion.

Later, I lie on the floor,
Exhausted by the fight to keep my sanity
amidst all the dread in my life, the panic that overwhelms.
I pull myself up, clutching your shirt,
My nose buried deep, tears still streaming down my face.
I place your shirt on my pillow, waiting for me tonight,
So my dreams will be of you, next to me,
Knowing it will make the morning harder,
But not caring, not right now, not this moment.
This moment is missing you, and it goes on forever.

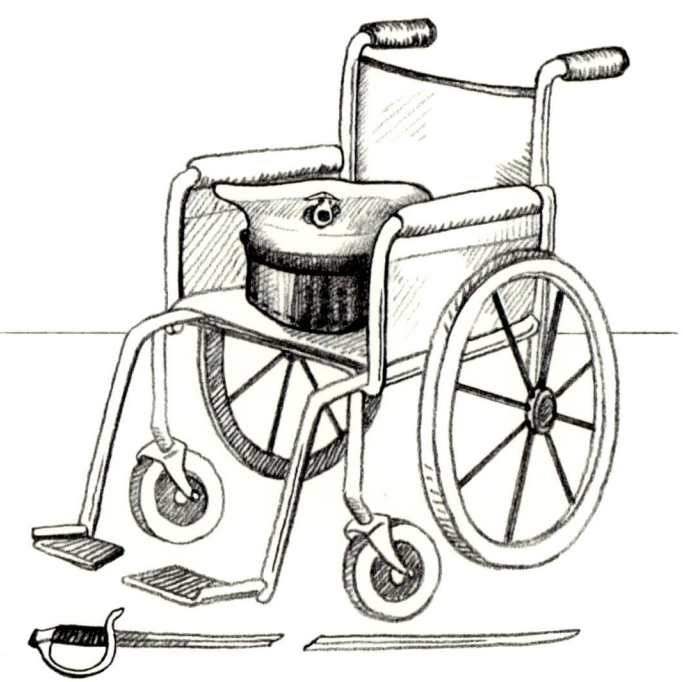

DREAM DESTROYED

I can only imagine your pain.
You worked for this, and went against all of us to gain this.
Though I wasn't happy when you chose this road,
Neither am I happy now.
I know you are hurting,
And my first instinct is to take away the pain.
I can't.
This is tearing me up inside.
I was made to stop the hurt,
To heal.
And I can't.
Words are not enough, I know.
Let me hug you,
Encircle you in my arms,
And I will protect you from the world outside.
If only for a while.

FIRST SNOWFALL

It starts slow,
quiet,
gentle.
They come down one by one,
one here, one there.
Suddenly a breeze kicks up and the flakes come down in groups,
Groups of three or four, but still
slowly, quietly, and
gently.
Then, with quickness amazing to see, the world is whited out,
Trees and buildings
simply dark shapes.
The flakes are no longer
slow, nor gentle,
and the wind is not quiet.
For some time it continues,
And I watch out the window as the birds at the feeders depart
for thicker cover.
The cats scurry to their boxes,
Not liking the cold wetness that sticks to
their fur.
Slowly, the flakes
stop.
The wind continues,
And now the flakes already fallen are whirling and dancing.
I sigh,
close the curtains,
and make plans for shoveling
in the morning.

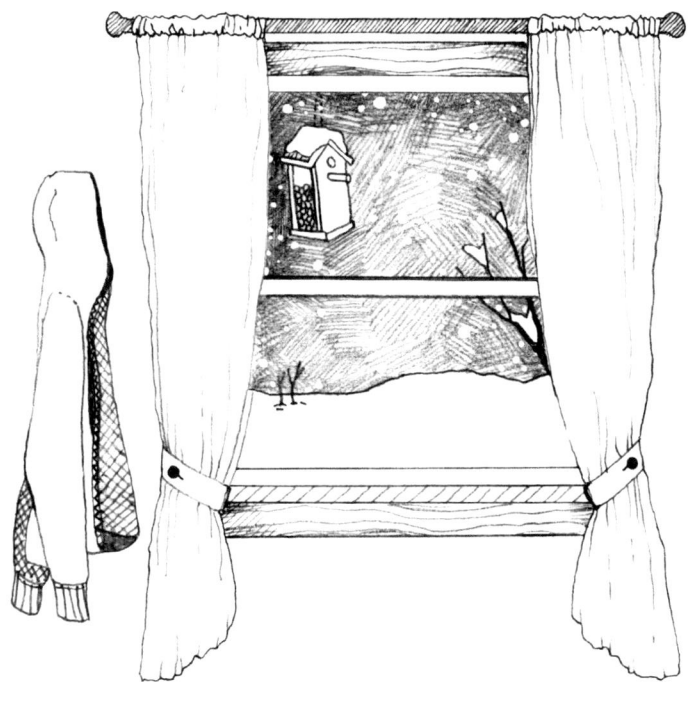

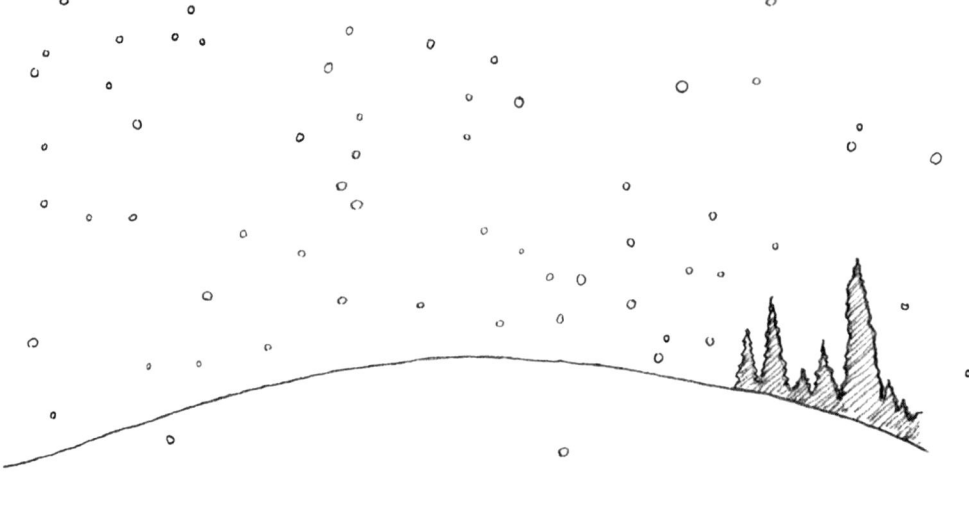

CABIN FEVER

Restlessness roams my brain.
I search, but nothing.
Where is it?
What am I looking for?
What is this fire coursing through my soul,
Molten emotion, causing false starts.
As a child, I ask –
Is it here yet?
No one answers.

WHAT IS LEFT

How do we know?
Mothers know everything, right?
We play with you,
dress you, feed you, and clothe you.
Care for you.
And little by little,
We learn to let go.
Our identity is you.
When you go,
What is left?
Are we nothing more
than hollow shells,
Filled with memories?
We are mothers forever,
But you go from children
to adults.
What is left for us?

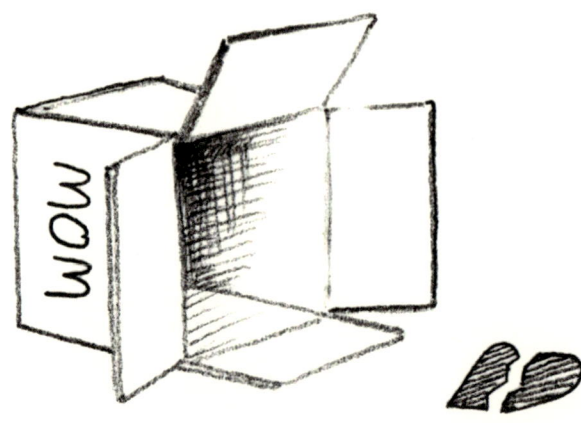

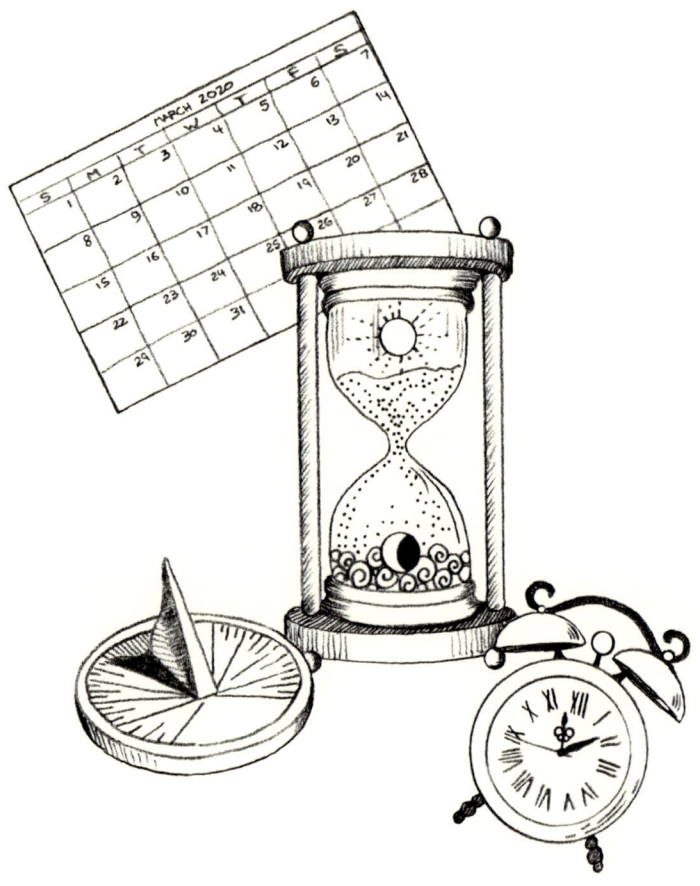

TIME

It slips into the past
without a backward glance;
Hurrying on its way and
shoving us ahead.
We dig in our feet,
But to no avail.
There is no stopping
this river of time,
No damming the onrush.
We are less than leaves
on the waves,
Less than the foam that
rides serenely at the top.
Time pays us no mind,
We do not exist for it.
They say there's never
enough time;
I say there's too much.

REMEMBERING THE PAST

As I look fondly on the tousled head,
I think of a small bundle in a basket
beside the bed, not so long ago.
And I smile, remembering.

As I wave good-bye to an eager five-year-old,
I think of how small he still is (to me).
And I smile, remembering.

As I kiss my new daughter,
I think how it was only yesterday he hated girls.
And I smile, remembering.

Today, as he looks
at my still form in the casket,
I hope he smiles,
Remembering.

TWILIGHT IS A STRANGE LIGHT

Twilight is a strange light,
Neither daytime nor nighttime;
Twilight is a strange light.

What kinds of things grow in twilight?
Strange and convoluted shapes,
Writhing across our vision?
Or straight and narrow,
Regimented in rows?

Twilight is a strange light.
What scent do we come across in twilight?
Is it wonderful, like rich roses in bloom?
Or heavy, dank, smelling of crushed earth and blood?

Twilight is a strange light.
What taste crosses our tongues in twilight?
Do we taste heavy, cloying blood and sweat?
Or is it the nectar of the heavens that crosses our lips?

Twilight is a strange light.
What sound accosts us in twilight?
Fairy bells, tinkling like water across stones?
Or screams of the accursed, banging at our eardrums with dwindling breath?

Twilight is a strange light.
What do our hands, our bodies, touch in twilight?
Do we feel the damp, sweaty flesh of living monsters,
Grabbing us up as we feel their teeth mangle our bodies?
Or do we feel softness, a kitten's fur, a soft-petaled flower?

Twilight is a strange light.
Twilight is both dusk and dawn,
The marker at each end,
Between the brightness of the day and
the darkness of the night.
The time of doorways,
of gateways,
of passage ways.
Twilight is a strange light,
Neither light nor dark;
Twilight is a strange light.

A MOTHER'S QUESTIONS

A mother does her best,
But always second-guesses.
Should she have done more?
Less?
What worked?
What didn't?
What should she have done?
Questions, always questions.
When is enough
enough?
When do you say,
"I'm done. You're on your own."
Do all mothers feel this way?
Or only the failures?
The joy at birth, the anguish at
letting go.
Untie now? Or hang on
a little longer.
Questions, always questions.

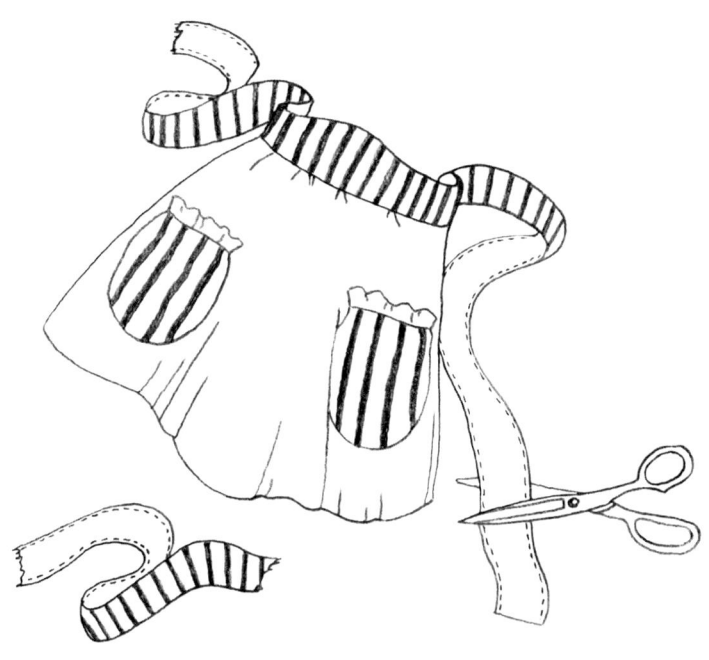

CROWDED

When I go outside
at night
and look up –
I am not alone.
Flashing lights cross
the stars
and leave me feeling –
Very crowded.
Where can I go
to be by myself?
Everywhere I look,
There are signs
of people.
Does the creator
look down
as I look up
and wonder
the same?

www.foxpointepublishing.com/author-paula-morhardt

https://www.facebook.com/authorpaula.morhardt

author.paula.morhardt@gmail.com